WITHIN

and

WITHOUT

Poems

JAMES RICHARD HANSEN

authorHOUSE

AuthorHouse™
1663 Liberty Drive
Bloomington, IN 47403
www.authorhouse.com
Phone: 833-262-8899

Published by AuthorHouse 08/01/2017

ISBN: 978-1-5462-0255-4 (sc)
ISBN: 978-1-5462-0254-7 (e)

Library of Congress Control Number: 2017911931

Print information available on the last page.

This book is printed on acid-free paper.

Contents

Love Poems to Kristen

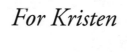

For Kristen

Dawn

Morning,
announced in dew and half-light,
haze and crisp air,
arrives.
My senses tingle.
Every nuance of tree and flower,
breeze and glittering light,
shows the way to freedom.

Oceanic Events

Sounds of the sea
echo through my inner world.
Waves of thoughts and memories
cascade before my mind's eye,
while dolphins swim with my feelings.
Intuitions and sensations
are swept up in the tide
and wash ashore
on the beach of consciousness.
My observer soars with gulls
and sees that I'm okay.

Finding My Stride

The moon plays silver harmonies
as a choir of stars sings
to the queen of the night.
Wisps of clouds frame and focus.
I walk beneath the Milky Way
in a cool breeze, finding my stride
in a poetic dance with darkness,
a dance I will continue in my sleep.

A Calling

I stand on shore amid the sibilance of the sea,
water crashing and rushing over sand and rock
as I imagine a long voyage in search of my grail.
Am I called to this voyage by the Pacific,
with its rhythmic undulations and shimmering blue?
Or am I called by my grail, or my grave, or God,
or the universe, or something inside me,
something always there but barely noticed
in the depths of my mind?

Rebirth

Carried by a calm breeze,
a whisper wafts through my open window.
The sound dies in my ears,
its vibrations spent.
Somewhere a new whisper
prepares to enter my home.
As I wait, I detect
the rustling of a tree,
its voice dying and reborn
in the same wind that soon will bring
another tranquil tone to my ears.

Serpent

Sunrise lies to me
in blinding orange.
I expect a good day,
but discover a serpent
under a stone.
My futility is futile.

As night approaches,
the fight almost over,
I wonder if tomorrow
will bring another lie,
another serpent.

Catharsis

The sunset flames red,
the sun flashes green
as it dips below the horizon.
Waves stroke the shore,
shuffling seaweed and sand.
Pink clouds drift with the wind.
The surrounding beauty
tears me from my troubles.
I want to soar with the gulls
and view the majesty from the sky.
My catharsis has begun.

Imagination

The warmth of the wood fire
drifts across my body.
Saffron flames flicker
through the windows of the stove,
their tongues darting and dividing,
creating a menacing menagerie
in a mad dance of transformation.
The surrounding darkness
centers my attention on the fire.
In the mysterious center,
the flames are creating hell,
but only for the wood.
I try to imagine
being in that inferno, but can't.
I start to think of all the people
who have burned,
but some inner block stops me
before I go too far.
Imagination can be wicked.

Flight

Day becomes night,
and my flight through the stars
slows. I fall to Earth, and sleep.
Deep in my dreams I fly once again
through the endless universe,
only to wake in my bed
to the sound of rain.

Inward Journey

As night looks through glass doors,
our torchiere lamp casts an eerie glow,
while the pothos plant forms an ominous shadow.
Lights, plants, and furniture create bizarre chiaroscuro
on the walls and floor.

I look inward
like a spelunker on my perennial journey into the abyss.
I feel a little sorry for myself.

Reconciliation

Silence stabs
in a storm of loss and loneliness.
Somewhere there is respite—
where the gentle sounds of friendship
push the quiet into the distance.

I stop ruminating and look outside,
where snow covers the darkness
with a veneer of purity.
But how can one reconcile
black and white,
silence and song?

Death's Glow

Fire flies into the skies
as trees struggle
for air and life.
They find only pain,
death.
I feel their fate
only from a distance.
Death glows orange,
then stabs the eyes
with black.
But years later,
saplings begin to reach
for the same skies
that took the ghosts
of their fathers.

Not Me

Rain spatters pavement,
creating watery music in the night.
As I listen, I drift with the water
running down the street
and wish I could feel
like rain for a moment,
or a rose,
or a lion.
I look up at the clouds
in the night sky
glowing from the city lights,
and I think,
what is it like to be up there,
preparing to fall,
to help a rose grow,
or provide a drink for a lion,
or make watery music?
What is it like to be rain
spattering pavement in the night?
What is it like not to be human,
not to be me?

Two Paintings

Nature paints in chiaroscuro
with moonlight and shadows.
The pattern differs now,
the walnut tree gone for a year.
Pines and oaks reach like tentacles
to the ocean of night.
Silhouettes of stray cats
prowl the driveway,
and a shooting star
creates a small streak of day.
When the sun bursts into morning,
it will destroy this work of art,
but will create another in realism
which, in time, will disappear itself.

Expanse

Pines look down on my writing,
peeking past the peach tree
that guards the lower half
of our property.
The walnut tree to the left,
with its dead, bare branches,
reaches for the sky
in lifeless longing.
In the distance, telephone lines
split the natural scene,
divorcing tree from tree,
branch from branch,
like marital divorces
separating one branch of life
from another.
Yet the entire scene
is covered by the clear sky,
the endless ethereal expanse,
unifying all that is under it.

Indelible

The sun burns a blinding path of light
from horizon to shore.
Light clouds glow pink and rose,
sea lies nearly motionless,
azure paints endless sky.

Protean clouds revise the heavens,
the Pacific taps the shore,
sea and sky lose light
as the sun slides away
and leaves a memory
as indelible as the stars.

Sleep?

The light drumbeat of rain
outside my bedroom window
makes me sleepy.
I finally stop resisting.
In my dreams I still hear the sound of rain,
but I'm in a dark forest near a stream.
I drink the cool, fresh water.
I lie down to nap
and wake in my bed.

Attending the Symphony

I wake from dreams of music
to a symphony of color
visible through the glass door.
Sunlight dances on the flowers and leaves
and sets our garden on fire.
Iridescent dewdrops sparkle,
creating hundreds of tiny rainbows.

The orchestra performs daily.

Other Languages

Notes fall on my ears,
played by the fire
in its dry, airy style.
It is a chorus of notes
that aren't notes,
like the music in everything
that sings without instruments.
A fire communicates
in its own language.
All I need to do is
open my mind and senses.

Impulse

Wind whistles through pines
that split the night.
The rising moon,
beautiful beyond vision,
shows me trembling trees
as God teaches me
the child's art of wonder.
Wispy streaks of cirrus
stretch across the sky.
My spirit soars
to the heavens
as my imagination
follows my impulse
toward the infinite.

Iridescent Sunset

The rippling surface of the Pacific
glows like a psychedelic mirror
as the falling fireball coats it with light.
Seagulls soar,
waves roll lightly to shore,
and blue sky fades,
leaving the moon's sliver of silver.
With the advent of stars,
my spirits surge like the tide.

Play

Playing at life,
I lose the playground
and my way.
I don't realize
the dangers or traps
that threaten me.
But whoever sets these traps
has no power
over my guardian angel,
who pulls me out,
dusts me off,
and sends me back to play.

Mozart

Time sang
through my tape player today.
Soft pillows under my head
matched those inside,
fluffed by the orchestra.
Fresh air played its song
through my window
and rose with the composer,
while the simplicity of the melodies
and the complexity of the harmonies
helped me breathe.
Tingling in my spine
accompanied the natural high.
But Mozart's secret was not revealed,
so I treated the experience
like a great meal that
I don't know how to cook,
won't put on pounds,
and will improve my mind.
I'll never be finished.

Progression

Stars and moon were out last night,
looking down on me as I walked,
stick in hand to fight off stray dogs.
Chill air and moonlight,
clear sky and starlight.
As day breaks now, stars have faded,
the chill has reached its coldest,
and the moon has disappeared
behind the mountains.
Dawn convinces me there is something
to look forward to,
another day of caring for Dad,
another day of living.

Seeing

I watch turquoise waves
spilling over each other,
azure skies framing the scene,
billowing clouds snaking and sneaking
across the seascape.
I feel I'm a part of it,
the millions of years of history,
the indelible mark in time.

But it's only a painting.

Awareness

Under the sun, undone
and weary of the dreary day,
I walk to the lake
and wake my senses.
Alert, I look inside.
After a long search,
I find the daily grind
has stolen my life.
To save my sanity,
I take a break
and lie on the sandy beach,
indulging my vanity
under the sun.

Waking

Day begins with a gift from the sky.
As cool drops fall on my upturned face,
I spread the rain over my skin,
massage my forehead and cheeks,
and feel the soothing moisture waking me.

The Mirror

The mirror is cracked.
Someone decided
he didn't like what he saw.
The cracks are iridescent,
as if the mirror were showing
all my sides at once.
They change like a chameleon,
but the mirror seems to exist in limbo,
at once dead *and* alive.
When this house is destroyed,
will the mirror cease to exist?
If only it could be reborn
as a talisman
for another lost soul.

Internal Itinerary

Undulating hills are covered
by black skies,
dark as my fears had been.
But now my mind is a zephyr.
During daylight I am lost,
but night is a map
for my escape
into nocturnal nothingness.
Do I see that void
in the night sky,
or is the scene inside me?
I find myself wishing
for a time machine,
or an augur's vision,
but only if the future
would be cloudless,
or at least not harsh.

Silhouettes

Stars surround the moon and its icy halo,
while white wisps slide across the sky
in a dim parade separating the stars.
I see silhouettes of trees and mountains,
signs of nighttime nature
that helps the world sleep.
As I watch, I think of daytime,
knowing that the silhouettes I see now
will leap into the sky tomorrow
with no hint of the laziness
of the night before.

Peace

The solemn moon fills me
as I walk in the cool night,
pale clouds visible in the silver light.
A gentle breeze soothes my skin
beneath countless stars.

I often look to the heavens for peace,
but find it within.

Night

The day collapses before my eyes,
a failure.
I handle it well, teary and slumping.
I go to bed praying for angels,
but demons infest my dreams.
The only angel to appear
is morning.

Morning

Sunrise nudges me awake,
peeling away the darkness of my dreams
and revealing the prize of a new day.
I let my nightmares go
and embrace the dawn
with a freshness drawn
from the depths of my soul,
as I rise to claim my prize.

Love Poems to Kristen

The Gift

I

Your eyes glow like sapphires,
and your golden hair
was born of your heart.
Your voice tastes like honey,
and your mind is a star.
I feared my rust and stone
would damage your treasures,
but you pulled me from the pit.
And now I am free to be.

II

I am transfixed
by your beauty.
The stars chart your life—
I want to sail the night sky.
Knowing you
Is salvation.

III

I think of you
my dreams soar
my heart yearns
my body turns
to fire.
I scream for you in the night
but my thirst cannot be quenched.
Drown me in your love.

IV

The setting sun glows
in adoration of creation.
But I notice only a flicker
in the corner of my eye,
for you will soon be here,
and my heart burns
with the heat of a thousand suns.

V

Night after night,
mutual love and lust
lead to total immersion
in a sea of passion,
a crescendo,
an endless symphony
of unparalleled ecstasy.
Tina Turner was wrong.
Love does have something to do with it.

VI

Life with you is a garden of love,
its life flowing inexorably through my veins.
Nothing could stop the power,
the inevitable push through the gates of destiny
into your arms.

Limits

I can't capture the essence of dew
or its iridescence in sunlight.
I can't know the mind of a crow
as it flies, or see from its eyes.
I can't comprehend
the infinite genius of humanity,
or its infinite folly.
I can't see beyond this life.

I can't know you perfectly,
though I want to passionately—
to love you more, if that's possible.

In Your Gaze

Moonlight fell from the sky
as I looked in your eyes
and saw the silver glow
grow in your gaze.
For months afterward
I remembered your purity
in the moonlight,
your loving look
spellbinding
like the full moon.

The life of Kelton Killer (Kel) shows a boy going through his life in Texas as it stretches to Washington, DC. He is taught to play the piano, which greatly enhances his life everywhere he goes as he is quite talented. When he attends college in Austin, he is further taught by a master of music, which takes him from just a good piano player to a master musician. On his first day in class, Kel meets three girls who are studying law. They form a group and help each other become lawyers.

After they pass the bar, they form a law office. They are helped by an alcoholic lawyer who they help sober up, and he guides them to becoming a prestigious law firm. The war takes Kel to Washington, where he serves three presidents. The story has several exciting adventures, with some love in the mix.

WILLIAM POST is the author of several novels of a variety of genres. Many are westerns as this book is, but he has World War I and World War II as well as the Civil War stories. Post was raised in West Texas was educated at Texas A.& M. and served in the U. S. Navy. After his service he became a surveyor for the Southern Pacific Railroad. This took him to the wilds of Texas, New Mexico, Arizona and California, where he learned the lore of those areas.

Post is licensed as a civil engineer and surveyor with the state of California. He retired as the Chief Engineer of the Long Beach Water Department. Taking an early retirement he began his writing career. Post is an Evangelic Christian and this thread is seen throughout the fabric of his stories. He now lives in Las Vegas, Nevada with his wife and extended family.

authorHOUSE®

ISBN 978-1-5462-0419-0

51399

9 781546 204190

Interplay

We play beautiful harmonies with the music of our lives.
We write love notes with our eyes.
Our embraces take us high.
Our words never lie.

Rendezvous

Stretched across the great expanse of white,
the lovers kiss.
In the dark hotel room,
they become a poem of their love.

Treasures

You are fine crystal in myriad colors and shapes.
Your kindness is a quiet mountain stream.
Your patience is a favorite pillow.
Your love is like the Louvre,
timeless,
sharing treasures with the world,
but most of all with me.

Let me be your wellspring of joy.
Let me be your eternal flame.
Let me be the keeper of your heart
and the curator of your soul
on our journey through
this priceless world.

Birthday 2009

Opposites

I see you in my dreams,
radiant as a double star.
Lilies cover the field where you stand,
white dress waving in the wind.

I walk toward you
in black jeans and black shirt,
restless as a devil.

I imagine our bodies and lives
entwined.

We lie in the lilies
and dream of our future
while the stars count us.

Birthday 2010

Celebration

I see you in the morning,
lightly touched with dew,
glowing in the half-light of dawn,
lighting the world with your radiance.

As you celebrate your birthday,
celebrate yourself,
as I do.

Birthday 2011

Ten Years Of Falling

I fall for you again and again.
I fall every time we kiss or embrace.
I fall for your beauty, your mind,
but especially your heart.
I fall as I did ten years ago—
in a rush of excitement and hope,
love and lust,
fascination and fantasy.
And I fall in anticipation
of our future together
which, though it's hard to believe,
will be even better.

Our Tenth Anniversary

Reverie

Just in time for sunset,
I stroll down the beach waiting for the green flash
you told me about when I moved here.
It's low tide, the sky is blue
with scattered, wispy clouds,
and cool wind blows inland from the Pacific.
My bare feet walk on cold, wet sand.

The sun nears the horizon,
so I stop and stare in that general direction.
I think of the time ten years ago
when you told me about the green flash.
I see the ten precious years
pass by my mind's eye.
Though you are miles away,
I see your face, your sparkling blue eyes,
your smile that warms me to my core.
I lose myself in reverie
about our thousands of wonderful moments together.

Finally, my mind drifts back to the sun,
but it's already down.
If there was a green flash, it's gone.
But the idea was enough.

Valentine's Day 2016

Seasons

It doesn't matter if autumn leaves fall
and decay on the ground,
or if the trees are bare in winter
and show no life until spring.
All that matters is our endless summer.

Birthday 2017

Printed in the United States
by Baker & Taylor Publisher Services